C000134997

Flight of the Quetzal

poems by

Evangeline Sanders

Finishing Line Press
Georgetown, Kentucky

Flight of the Quetzal

ACKNOWLEDGMENTS

Special thanks to the following publications, in which early versions of some of these poems first appeared:

Sky Island Journal: "Landmarks", "De Todo Corazón"
I Am a Furious Wish: Anthology of Lowcountry Poets: "Red", "Fragments: Chiquimula, Guatemala"

Publisher: Leah Huete de Maines
Editor: Christen Kincaid
Cover Art: Rachel Greene Phillips
Author Photo: Anna Slabetska
Cover Design: Elizabeth Maines McCleavy

Order online: www.finishinglinepress.com
also available on amazon.com

Author inquiries and mail orders:
Finishing Line Press
PO Box 1626
Georgetown, Kentucky 40324
USA

Table of Contents

To the people of Guatemala, with love

Flight of the Quetzal

(How the Quetzal Got Its Red Belly)
The Battle of El Pinar, Guatemala, 1524

According to tradition,
when the last K'iche Maya king heard the clatter
of a hundred Spanish hooves and heels,
the scrape of steel against steel,
he fastened his sandal straps and marched into battle
with a crown of quetzal feathers.

He clutched his wooden club
in a tight, brown fist as he stood
on the grasslands of El Pinar, gaze shifting to the sun
to watch his quetzal, his *nahual*,
glide through shafts and spheres of light,
settle on a rock with a snap of the wings,
tilt its head and cry.

And when he saw the great conquistador
mounted on his warhorse
with skins and sheathes of iron, the last K'iche Maya king
killed the horse and not the man

because he could not separate the horse
from the man, lacking the concept of
beast of burden.

According to tradition,
when the last K'iche Maya king shoved his club
into the soft hide of the beast, it staggered
and slumped to the ground,
slinging the great conquistador from its saddle.

And when he had sprung to his feet,
the great conquistador gathered up his shield and spear,
spun around and bared his teeth.
The quetzal hovered overhead, scanning the battlefield,
giving one last, desperate cry
as the great conquistador's spear pierced
the bare brown chest of the king.

According to tradition,
the bird fell silent as it landed in the grass
to dip its feathers in the blood
of the last K'iche Maya king.

There is another version of the legend,
lesser known.

According to tradition,
when Tecún Umán,
the last K'iche Maya king, heard the clatter
of a hundred Spanish hooves and heels,
he transformed into a quetzal and flew into battle
with rippling feathers, three crowns of gold.

De Todo Corazón

I

A pianist plucked a sheet from her binder,
propped it on the music shelf,
straightened out her skirt
as she cleared her throat,
tucked hair behind her ear.
We stretched our necks, standing
on tiptoes to glimpse our parents
perched on fold-up chairs
in the audience, cameras raised.

Twenty-four pairs of shoes
stomped on carpeted risers, spun around
and clapped, snapped and clapped and
spun around, paper chain necklaces
rustling with red, green,
white, strings of yarn and glitter,
hands thrown to the ceiling
on the opening chord of the
chorus. *Feliz Navidad.*

II

In those days, by the broom closet
in the back left corner
of the classroom, Spanish
was thumb-tacked posters
with bubble letters, clip art sombreros,
maracas, Mexican roses, cutout quetzals:
los colores, los días, los meses, el alfabeto.
Purple *martes*, bright yellow *sábado*,
fat and sleek, printed beside a sketch
of a sun with shades and a tennis visor.

A handful of Smarties and Silly Bandz
for anyone who could stand
and recite the alphabet all the way through,
rolling their *R*'s
with a wet flick of the tongue.

III

Spanish ripened like a papaya
in the seat by the fourth-floor window.
Fill-in-the-blank worksheets,
dog-eared textbooks (gently used),
vocabulary face-offs in front of the class.
A teacher with bright pink underpants,
a paper rose in his shirt pocket, a hand
on the shoulder of a girl with braces
and a purple backpack.

And then, years later,
Cervantes, Allende, Marquéz,
One Hundred Years of Solitude, Jungle Tales.
Banana plantations, imperial capitalism,
analyses of space and mood.
A gray Picasso painting with a Fascist bull
and wild-eyed horse, mouth
flung to the sky, screaming.

IV

My mother asks me the question
at a Mexican restaurant.
*You're afraid to speak to people
in Spanish. Why?*

I picture my friends from South America
who laugh, smile, slab tuna salad on
toasted bread, press their bodies together
on the picnic table
because they can smell home
on each other's skin.

The two-stanza, eight-line poem
I spent four hours writing
for my Hispanic Literature class
because I didn't know how
to forge something beautiful
from a language that wasn't my own.

I don´t know, I respond.
She shrugs, reaching for a chip.
Me neither.

V

Feliz Navidad, I tell the hostess
on our way out the door.
She smiles, waves. *Feliz Navidad.*

Our eyes meet, and my mouth
falls open to finish the blessing,
but she is already gone,
guiding another family to their table.

I whisper it to myself as I step
into the parking lot.

De todo corazón.

Landmarks

Volcán de Fuego
Eruption of June 3rd, 2018

Stack of charred rock, slit of sulfur—
stuffed with smoke and pellets,

cocked like a musket
on the shoulder of the valley.

Just southwest of Guatemala City
(12:00 P.M. local time), hot ash spills

from the summit in charcoal
plumes, swallows up trees

and truck tires, melts the rubber
into the dirt. Within minutes,

corn stalks and coffee plants
are slashed at the roots,

sloughed off the slopes, shoved
face-down into pyroclastic flow.

Oh, Volcán de Fuego, cocked and
oiled mosquete: did you notice

the red-bellied birds in the branches
(green spout of feathers, black-tipped

beaks tucked into breasts),
moments before you pursed your lips,

spat into the sun? The cows and
cloudless fields of sky, the corn husks

and fruit carts—mango skins
scattered like gold in the streets?

Iglesia Vieja

It stands in ruins, a scrap of colonial
fabric, slathered with moss and glue,

stretched over the frame of a city
choked by weeds, powerlines,

pink concrete cafes. In 1773,
an earthquake split the skin

of the streets, ripped through flesh
and muscle, shook blood

from the roofs of the cathedrals.
But the walls of Iglesia Vieja

remain—packed in place, a corridor
of columns and cracked stone,

bricks, prints of pineapples
and native birds. Tourists shuffle by

with their cameras and sunglasses,
pointing at the arches, the trees

that bend and stretch through
the rubble. Oh, Iglesia Vieja:

do you remember the hand
that pressed pen to parchment,

sketched the curves of your altar—
the men that slapped brick against brick,

chiseled a cold cross into stone,
hands folded in an Alleluia, Alleluia?

Guide to a Short-Term Mission Trip

(A Note From Your Mission Leaders)
Destination: Guatemala

Shopping for Attire

Clothes should be cotton, lightweight (there will be
      sheets of sweat, dirt, clinging to thighs, caking
heels with black grit). Guatemalan summers
      are hot, mud-slapped, swamped with rain and
mosquitoes, even in high-altitude villages. Sheathe
      the legs, smear sunscreen on the tops of the feet.
Prepare for hour-long hikes to huts, chafing,
      skin against skin. Natives weave bright
threads into shirts, twist them into vines and
      flowers—tiny, intricate petals, red and white,
wild roses and water lilies. Scan the clearance rack
      at Kohl's for skirts—any color, any pattern—
zig-zagged, striped, pleated or straight-cut. Sweatpants
      are allowed (baggy, full-length), but only around
the hotel. Remember: cover the legs.

Let us know if you have any further questions
      about attire.

Entering the Hotel Room

Spray down the sink, the shower, the toilet seat.
      Scrub with warm water and soap. Hotel rooms
are cleaned, swept, soaked in disinfectant, but it
      doesn't hurt to double-check, swipe a rag across
the surfaces. Shine a light under the mattress, search
      for stains, bed bugs. Normal hotel protocol.
Don't stick your face under the faucet (tap water
      will pump your intestines with parasites, bacteria).
Brush your teeth with bottled water, pour it over
      the bristles, swish with Listerine. Don't open your
mouth in the shower. Press your lips together, let
      the water dribble down your chin. Remember: lock
the doors when you leave.

Let us know if you have any further questions
about the hotel.

Practicing Cultural Sensitivity

Understand this: you are entering a country with
        an extensive history of bloodshed and oppression.
Cultural sensitivity is crucial. We all, as missionaries,
        have the privilege of sharing the Gospel—a bursting
of the heart, a swiping of the fingers across strings
        of salvation. Sing, laugh, cry with our brothers and
sisters in Christ. Clasp their hands like water lilies,
        crouch beside them and pray. God's provision
is like rain, soaking through soil, tapping on tin roofs,
        soothing and healing. Remember: we are not here
to injure or oppress, despite what others believe.
        We are here to encourage.

Let us know if you have any further questions
        about our mission.

The Interpreter

Mid-twenties, dark green
button-down and faded jeans,
brown leather flip-flops,
hands shoved into pockets.
Bible pinched in the pit
of his shoulder,
gold chain cross strung
around his collar.

He stands by the mango tree
and waves. *I will be your interpreter*
while we explore my hometown,
he says, smiling as we approach.
His English is slow, deliberate.

My name is José
and I love Jesus.

Fragments: Chiquimula, Guatemala

I

They speak, and the syllables
splash into their saucepans
like fish, wet and sizzling,
plump-scaled, pink-scaled,
gunky fins and flanks that drip
with balls of sweat and salt.

The *niñas chiquitas* giggle
when I place my hand on the
bubbling stovetop—when I squeal
and lurch backwards, pink flesh
pulsing, cheeks streaked
with soot and humiliation.

¡Mira la gringa! I can still feel
my heartbeat in my fingertips,
but they slap me on the back
and dip my hand in the
water basin, wrapping it with
stiff strips of tape, grinning
as we toss our tortillas.

II

I see a stump of bone, a slab
of red muscle and flesh,
crusted dry, flaking and peeling
around her kneecap—a splash
of blood, a speckle of ash.

She swats at the flies that
settle in the mush of the wound,
sighing and blotting her forehead,
blinking at the ants in the dirt
by her bare feet. *El hospital
está demasiado lejos,* she breathes.
Y nadie podía llevarme.

III

We stop by the gate
of the church, and he steps on
with his daughters, holding
their hands as he hoists them
into the bed of our truck.
He rubs their shoulders
and smiles, scraping
grass and mud off his boots.

The youngest daughter
grabs my arm and points
to the patchwork of fields.
Maiz, she says, motioning to
the yellow-green sprouts.
I nod.

She watches me, warm and
unblinking, fingering the rim
of her dress as we ride down
the mountain in the rain.

On Examining a Portrait of Pedro de Alvarado, The Great Conquistador

I wonder if they painted you
      in all your splendor,
            Pedro de Alvarado,

you god of sun
      and sword, clothed like a doll
            in cuffs and collars

of lace, hand on hip, fingers
      brushing the studs
            of your iron belt.

I wonder if they painted you
      in all your lightness,
            you seed of dawn,

when the warm, white rays
      had framed your form,
            flushed your cheeks

with blood, bathed
      the walls of the palace
            in rivers of light.

Even in those days,
      Pedro de Alvarado—
            when artists painted

over scars with smooth
      brush strokes, softened
            skin and veins, sculpted waists

with fine-edged pens—
      I wonder, even then,
            if they could capture

your beauty, oh great
        conquistador, God's anointed.
                The Spanish blue eyes, the

golden pleats of hair,
        the broad white hands,
                strengthened by a thousand

thrusts of the sword
        under a scarlet sun.

Centipede

You were the orange thread
that wrapped around the horn
of the dung beetle
in the cylinder of rubber bugs from Target
(a present for my fifth birthday).
My father snipped at the tape
with scissors, popped open the flaps
of the canister, dumped
the toy bugs onto the carpet—a tangle
of legs and antennae, twisted
together like wet vines.
My brother would dangle you
in my face, drape you over my arm
while I was asleep,
fling you onto my foot as I screamed
and slammed the bathroom door
in his face.

Oh, little thread
on the curb of the sidewalk,
curled and splayed after Guatemalan rain:
you look like a worm from a distance,
but I'm not fooled. I can see
the twin rows of legs, the black-shelled
body, the twitch and flick of the antennae.
If this land is your home,
ciempiés—if these streams are
your blood, these valleys
your vessels—my fear will not stand.
It will fall. It will sacrifice itself
to these hills.

If this land is your home, *ciempiés*—
I will count you
as another twisted thread
in the tapestry of a nation.

Sergio Eats Chocolate

It scuttles over the slab
of concrete (claws askew),
strapped at the girth with a
shoelace, eyes flicking
to the steam by the stove.

A small boy grips the string,
stands beside the door of the hut,
studies our shoes
as the crab picks
at brownish crumbs.

¿Cuál es su nombre? I ask,
pointing to the crab.
Sergio, he responds.
Le gusta comer chocolate.

Se Fue

I

Se fue (he/she left): conjugation of *irse* (to go away, to depart):
preterit tense, indicative mode,
third-person singular, reflexive, irregular. Used when the
destination

is unknown, unspecified.
Not to be confused with *ir* (to go),
its derivative,
also irregular,
also indicating movement,
almost always used in conjunction with the preposition *a*
and a destination.

II

Se fue, she says. Her husband
stares at her, murmurs something,
swipes a finger across her cheek.
Mi hija, she continues, shifting
her feet. *Se fue.*

¿Tu hija? we ask.
¿Se fue?

She glances over her shoulder
to the mountains.

Sí. Se fue.

Until the Land is Truly Free

During mating season, the male quetzal
parades its tropical plumage,

cooing, ruffling its feathers. Splashes
of dark blue, cyan, dripping down

the shoulders and spine, bleeding into
emerald, copper, green-gold.

Waxy yellow beak, gray-tipped wings.
Red blush of the belly. It shuffles its feet

and coos, scuttling along the branch,
peeking through the wet, glossy leaves

of the forest. Heart drumming to the beat
of some sad, ancient song.

Smooth, deep-bellied notes, repeating:
keow, kowee, keow, k'loo, keow, k'loo, keelo.

From March to May, these calls
can be heard in the canopies

after a rainfall, but for most of the year,
the quetzal squats on a branch, silent.

According to tradition, quetzals once filled
the forests with dazzling melodies

that swept through the hills
and valleys, flooded the fields with life.

According to tradition, they will not
sing again until the land is truly free.

Red

I

I set my passport on my lap
and unbuckle the leather wings,
tapping the page with the
rectangular stamp. It's
smudged around the edges,
red as a wound.

Guatemala.
Departed.
17.June.

II

Do you see the red?
Do you see the red that spreads
across the sky at dawn,
casts shadows onto the wings
of the plane?

Do you see it dissolving
the dark blue of night,
unfurling like a rose
from the inside-out, exposing
the warm underbelly of the world?

Blood red (dark, hot, metallic),
staining the backs
of the airplane seats. Yarn red,
scarlet, twisting and looping
through pinks and golds.
Mango skin red.

Quetzal belly red, like a
slice of the sky itself,
framing it all, shielding it all.

III

There is a country that is red.
I don't know it, but it is red,
and there is a song, and the song
is red. Somewhere above the plains
of El Pinar, suspended by the arms
of the sun, a quetzal circles
and sings, circles and sings.

Evangeline Sanders is an MFA student at the University of Alabama and a graduate of Clemson University, where she received degrees in Psychology and Spanish. Her poetry has been published in several literary journals, both print and online. She teaches undergraduate English classes and serves as an Assistant Editor for the Black Warrior Review in Tuscaloosa, Alabama.